LUCKY JOHNNY MILROY

Ramblings of an Old Man

By John R. Milroy

Lucky Johnny Milroy
Ramblings of an Old Man

Published by
Sarge Publications
866-878-2096

Book Design by
Angela Addington
Allegra Alpena
(formerly Model Printing Service)
829 W. Chisholm St.
Alpena, Michigan 49707
www.allegraalpena.com

ISBN 978-1-60307-314-1

DEDICATION

Written for
Joyce Ann Petersen Milroy

TABLE OF CONTENTS

Milroy Was There
By John R. Milroy
L Company, 376th Regiment
94th Infantry Division
KILROY WAS HERE
OLD MAN'S MEMORIES
LUCKY JOHNNY
As written by
John R. Milroy
OLD MAN'S MEMORIES
LUCKY JOHNNY MILROY
As written by
John R. Milroy

PREFACE

I am a unique author of four books. Why? Because I have spent thousands of dollars to have them published but have chosen to give away a majority for free, and more recently donate any proceeds from my latest book to the Hazelden Betty Ford Treatment Center. How did this unlikely idea begin?

Once I purchased my first computer in 2004, I saw how much easier the writing process could be and decided to look back on my life and create a memoir for my family. At 79 years of age, I saw that I had experienced many interesting and unusual things, led by my WWII experience in France, Germany, and Czechoslovakia from age 18 to 21. I believe that God not only played a role of keeping me safe in my life during WWII, but God also gave me a mind that still observes what is going on around me. Now at 96 in 2021, I can still remember my experiences. God also gave me a beautiful wife in Joyce Petersen Milroy and we were blessed with 67 years of marriage and four wonderful children. Joyce went to heaven at age 93 on April 19, 2021.

My first memoir is entitled Milroy Was There and was written while living in Alpena, Michigan. While writing, I sent drafts of the chapters to friends and young relatives, and all said the content was great and to "keep writing". Maybe they were just being kind to Grandpa. The book was printed by Allegra of Alpena, Michigan and then published in 2010 through Sarge Publications. I especially received significant help from Angela Addington with Allegra.

Part of that book dealt with WWII and what happened

when I returned home to Kalamazoo, Michigan. After WWII I returned to college at Western Michigan University. I had three objectives to be fulfilled in the following 3.5 years, having completed one semester before joining the army.

1. **Have fun**
2. **Use the G.I. Bill to pay for my education** – in addition, I received a letter for playing on the college tennis team which paid for all related costs including the wooden tennis racket.
3. **Graduate with honors from college**

I accomplished all three!

After the first book was published, I realized I was giving it away not only to my family but to many people I knew and didn't know that I encountered in our community. For example, I met exchange students from foreign countries such as Russia, Germany and the Czech Republic, as well as students from other states in the United States. All students that I met got an autographed copy. Also, my weekly fine dining at McDonalds with friends often resulted in genuine interest from strangers as I always wore my baseball cap that stated that I was a member of the 94th Division in WWII. Again, I did not charge a penny. I just enjoyed sharing and hearing their stories as well. I ended up giving away about 2,500 copies of my first book!

Joyce and I then moved from Alpena, Michigan to Saginaw, Michigan and the New Hope Valley West Independent Retirement Living Community. We lived there for 2 years and 7 months. During that time, I wrote a second book entitled Old Man's Memories, Lucky Johnny, published in 2020. At first, I considered selling them and had 450 printed in Alpena, but as it turned out I gave away all but a couple for free.

We then moved to Wescourt Independent Living in Saginaw, and it was there that I wrote a third book entitled Old Man's Memories, Lucky Johnny R. Milroy, published in 2021. This time I decided to sell the book through Amazon.com. A Kindle version was created for which I would receive $1.05 for each sale and a hard-cover book receiving .44 per book. The ease for potential buyers using Amazon intrigued me. I also decided any proceeds I did receive from this book would be donated to the Hazelden Betty Ford Foundation. Why? Let me share with you about my brother Bruce.

Bruce was 2 years and 4 months older than me, and we also had a younger sister Nancy. We first lived on Burnham Drive just blocks from the heart of Kalamazoo. I learned in 1988 at our mother's funeral that Bruce had started to drink while still a teen, something I was not aware of, but did know of his drinking as an adult. Ironically during WWII his assigned post in Brazil was arranging the parties for army officers, serving liquor and food, arranging bands and lining up chaperoned girls to dance with the men. After the war, Bruce then attended the University of Michigan, married, and began his family and work life. He continued to drink and often his wife, Bobbie, would call me in the evening to ask me to go to a bar, usually in a hotel, to get Bruce and bring him home safely. He would often get very angry at me, and I remember once I took off my glasses and said, "hit me" but he never did, and I always got him home safely.

Finally at age 49, Bruce decided to get help to stop drinking. I accompanied him on a plane for Minneapolis where when landing we were met by four representatives from Hazelden. Fortunately, from the time of leaving the clinic until his death, he no longer drank. He was an active member of Alcoholics Anonymous and a mentor to many people.

At the time of his rehab experience, it cost approximately $26,000. Bruce was fortunate enough to have the money, but I know many alcoholics have spent much of their money on alcohol, and may not have the funds needed, therefore my desire to help fund Hazelden in the memory of the success of my brother through their organization.

I end this Preface by sharing that writing these three, and now fourth books, has been so much fun and has brought great joy and experiences to my life. I have gotten to know many wonderful people through my books. The first Chapter of this book details the relationship I developed with Dr. Yvonne S. Thornton, even though we have never met face-to-face.

People is what it is all about. Another example of people I have met occurred in 2016. My daughter Jan was visiting and one day Joyce, Jan and I decided to visit the Fashion Square Mall in Saginaw. Joyce and I always enjoyed going to the mall, driving the 145 miles from Alpena to Saginaw. It had once been a vibrant place, but now due to changes in how people make purchases, often through the Internet, many malls like Fashion Square have seen a decline. It was sad for us to see.

Once inside I looked for a bench to sit on while Joyce and Jan did a bit of shopping. I happened to see a bench which was occupied by two ladies and I joined them. They were a mother and daughter and we spent time getting to know one another. Hazel is retired but Gena is a very busy attorney in Saginaw. It was so enjoyable, and I gave them one of my books. And although we haven't seen each other since due to COVID we have maintained contact through notes and over the phone, and I consider them cherished friends. Again, through sharing my book I was able to meet these wonderful people.

I genuinely believe that my stories, especially about alcohol-recovery and mental health problems can be a help to someone. In Chapter Two I write about knowing a gentleman with dyslexia and hope others will learn as I have about this condition.

I believe my stories are interesting, sincere and could help many readers. I am grateful for the many experiences I have had through the writing of these books.

Reference:

Hazelden Betty Ford Foundation
www.hazeldenbettyford.org

Alcoholics Anonymous
www.aa.org

CHAPTER ONE

Dr. Thornton, M.D., Author of <u>The Ditch Digger's Daughters</u>

I will start with sharing a special relationship I have developed with an extraordinary person, Dr. Yvonne S. Thornton of now Hackensack, New Jersey. As I mentioned in my Preface, we have yet to meet face-to-face.

I learned of Dr. Thornton through a memoir she had written that I happened to come across in Borders Books (now out of business) in Ann Arbor, Michigan.

First let me say that Dr. Thornton's life history is extensive, impressive and inspiring. As stated on her web site, doctorthornton.com, "She is a double-Board Certified specialist in obstetrics, gynecology and maternal-fetal medicine. She has risen to the academic rank of Emeritus Professor of Obstetrics and Gynecology. She is a member of the Association of Women Surgeons, a life member of The New York Academy of Medicine, and is a Fellow of the American College of Obstetricians and Gynecologists and the American College of Surgeons. Her biography is presently in Who's Who in America and Who's Who in the World. She has been listed in The Best Doctors -- New York Metro Area. She was also listed in New York Magazine as one of the Top Ten Maternal-Fetal Medicine Specialists in New York City.

Doctor Thornton was the first black woman in the United States to be Board Certified in High-Risk Obstetrics and to be accepted into The New York Obstetrical Society."

To read much more about this extraordinary woman,

just go to doctorthornton.com.

As I mentioned our family often stopped at Borders Books before attending University of Michigan football games. (We originally became season ticket holders in 1974 via a kind parting gift from my boss the President of the First National Bank of Ft. Dodge, Iowa Earl Underbrink as we prepared to move to Alpena, Michigan.)

One Saturday in 2011 we were making our usual trip to Borders before a game, and we saw a sign on the door reading, "Last Saturday to buy books here. We are closing." We were shocked. It was that trip where I saw a book entitled Something to Prove, A Daughter's Journey to Fulfill a Father's Legacy by Dr. Thornton published in 2010. I purchased it and enjoyed it so much I sent her a letter of congratulations and I included my memoir, Milroy Was There.

A few weeks later when returning home from a McDonald's meeting with friends, Joyce met me at the door and said Dr. Thornton had called. Joyce didn't realize who that was and therefore was worried I had missed some medical appointment. Nope, it was my soon to be new friend!

I called the Doctor back and in talking she asked if I had also read her first book, The Ditch Digger's Daughters, published in 1995. In 1997, it was made into a movie for television! I hadn't, but of course I then did read it and again so enjoyed it. Our friendly phone conversation ended with her saying, "I am putting you on my Christmas list". That December a letter arrived with the envelope addressed to me in beautiful calligraphy and each December since I have received these special letters.

In addition to the telephone the Doctor and I have exchanged written notes and letters. In a note from January 2021, she thanked me for sending her my second book and her note read, "I am enjoying it immensely." She also included a warm note after learning of Joyce's passing in April of 2021. She wrote, "you are a remarkable person with a loving family" and signed it with warm regards. We have become warm, caring friends. I respect her so much for what she has accomplished in her life and especially the impact it has had on and for women.

This is just one of many examples of new friends I have discovered through sharing my books and gives you an idea why I have enjoyed spending the money to produce them and am not concerned about receiving any revenue. I hope I meet Dr. Thornton or a member of her family some day before I meet my beautiful Joyce in Heaven.

CHAPTER TWO
Dyslexia

I first became aware of Dyslexia in 1970 when I was Vice President of Nazareth College in Kalamazoo, (where I had the pleasure of working for three years for the wonderful Sister Mary Bader who was President of the College from 1962 to 1974.) One of the Nazareth College teachers was learning about the Dyslexia condition to help students at the college.

Years later I had a more personal experience meeting Bob, a 90-year-old at the New Hope Retirement Community in Saginaw, Michigan. Bob and I would often watch movies together in the small theater New Hope had for their residents and sometimes we'd stay and discuss the film and then our lives. Bob told me he had Dyslexia and that coupled with Macular Degeneration, he could not easily read or write. However, it was obvious that his intelligence with mechanical things was extraordinary. I found this fascinating. He told me that his parents didn't graduate from high-school, and they lived in a secluded residence, with the nearest neighbor a quarter of a mile away and he

had few childhood friends. Despite his condition he served successfully in the Marine Corp, took advantage of the G.I. Bill and attended Lane Technical College, and then worked for 30 years with a large manufacturing company that made farm equipment.

After we moved to Wescourt Retirement I then had the unexpected pleasure of meeting Bob's daughter Paula. Paula's parents are divorced and her mother lives at Wescourt. Paula visits and cares for her mother every day after spending the morning on an outing with her father usually looking for antique treasures in unlikely places. Bob now lives in an apartment. Paula and her husband are retired General Motors mechanical engineers and it has been a pleasure knowing her.

I also met another senior resident of New Hope who I will call "Sally" and she shared she had Dyslexia but her wealthy parents were able to look for help from Boston hospitals when she was just seven years old. She was fortunate enough to receive training on how to deal with the condition and she went on to receive a college degree and became a minister of a church near Boston. She then moved to Saginaw to serve as a chaplain of a hospital here. Unfortunately, in her early 60s she suffered a stroke and is now recovering at New Hope.

I found the stark differences in Bob and "Sally's" stories to be profound and it caused me to want to write about this condition and share that help is out there. For more information reference the Dyslexia Foundation at dyslexiafoundation.org.

CHAPTER THREE
"Big Grandma" Nora Schoonmaker

My grandmother Nora Schoonmaker, on my mother's side, was an important guide and influence in my life. Nora and her husband John Ray, a pharmacist, had three children: my mother Norda, a son Carl and another daughter Marian. "Big Grandma" as we called Nora, apparently separated from her husband at some point, and in fact I never met him. She ended up owning and living in a three-story house with her mother-in-law and accepted and welcomed boarders who were usually female students from the near-by Western Michigan College of Michigan in Kalamazoo. Now known as Western Michigan University.

I have such wonderful memories of time with my grandmother at her home. When the college students were away for Christmas break our family of five, my parents Bob and Norda, my brother Bruce, sister Nancy and me, spent the week sleeping in the vacant bedrooms, enjoying meals, the holiday festivities and exploring the outside neighborhood, much of which was the college grounds.

"Big Grandma" would often have me there for lunch during the school year and tried to teach me to play the piano. I also helped her willingly with chores around the house such as mowing the lawn and climbing trees to pick fruit. Although the family history about my grandfather, John Ray, is a bit murky, it appears through internet research that he died in his 50's of a heart problem. Later in her senior years Nora moved to the Marlborough Apartments in downtown Kalamazoo near the Kalamazoo Art Institute and I visited her often there.

Grandma never said a bad word about another person. She was active managing her home, caring for her mother-in-law and the college girls. She was active in a Methodist Church, singing in the choir and composed church music that was sung there. She also learned to play the cello later in life. She was kind, talented and an intelligent lady who often beat her neighbors playing chess. She never made fun of others. She was a serious woman though and I almost never saw her laugh or cry. She was a mentor for me and a role model for senior citizens. I am sure she was proud of her family, and she never spoke badly of anyone, including her estranged husband.

I admired her for taking care of herself and her family and the way she lived her life.

CHAPTER FOUR
France during WWII: Saint Nazaire and Lorient

Marshalling area for the St. Nazaire Sector forces in the vicinity of Châteaubriant

While I was in Europe during WWII, we infantrymen were never given any maps, nor could we read the road signs in other languages to help us determine our location. Only our superiors had that information. We didn't know what the specific goals were or the mission of the 94th Division. We were told where to go and what to do. It was just the way it was. So now looking back and reading more information it is fascinating to me to know what was really going on.

In addition to reading, I was blessed to meet Matt and Rhonda Mulroy. We met in New Orleans in 2013 at a 94th Division Reunion. Matt's father, now deceased, was in the 94th Division (although not in my same Company Unit) and both Matt and Rhonda have become avid students in learning everything they can about his father's experiences. They have also been to Europe to see where his father was during the war.

One example of the new perspectives I have now involves when we were in France for 3 months in 1944. We did not engage in much fighting. We primarily went on day and night patrols to stay informed on where the Germans were and if they had moved. Occasionally, a German soldier or two would surrender to us. While there our Division had 15,000 troops stationed with half near the Saint Nazaire harbor, one of the largest ports of the Atlantic coast of France, and the other half of our troops were outside Lorient, France. I have since learned that there were 55,000 Germans located just 91 miles north of us and that an extensive German Submarine base was located at Lorient. Approximately half of the German troops were located at Saint Nazaire and the other half at Lorient, France. The Germans were massed there to protect these important harbors as places to repair their submarines.

Headed for Germany, on 40+8 cars, pup tents at Chateaubriant, Fr. Passed Chartes, France on train.

These 40+8 trains are what we rode to Germany in.

They could hold 40 men or 8 horses.

Matt Mulroy has visited that area and saw the thick cement walls and ceilings of the bunkers where the Germans stayed, and it was clear why many of the U.S. air-craft bombs did not have much success. We had no idea at the time of the significance of the harbors or how many more troops the Germans had compared to us.

Although we saw little fighting or war in France during that time, we later did experience more difficult conditions when we crossed into Germany during the winter of 1944/1945. In addition to fighting, we experienced record-breaking minus zero temperatures with piles of snow. Many soldiers received frost-bitten feet. I was fortunate enough to not experience that.

Again, even in Germany we did not know the strength or status of the German army as we were not told anything. It has been interesting to look back on what we went through with a more informed eye.

John R. Milroy as a young soldier

CHAPTER FIVE
Parochial Schools Advantage Over Public Schools

My siblings and I all attended public schools in Kalamazoo. Only my brother Bruce's wife, Bobbie went to a private Catholic school. The history of public and parochial schools is an interesting one. In 1858 on South Westnedge near Vine St. the first public high school in Kalamazoo was opened. Then fifteen years later an important lawsuit was set in motion. The structure is still standing, and a plaque stands on the outside which highlights the case. It reads:

> **"Near here, in 1858, Kalamazoo's first high school was opened. Fifteen years later the right of the school board to levy taxes to support a high school was challenged. A unanimous decision of the Michigan Supreme Court, rendered by Justice Thomas M. Cooley in 1874, affirmed an opinion of Kalamazoo Circuit Judge Charles R. Brown that upheld this right. As a result, the way opened for free high schools in Michigan and also in other states."**

In Michigan, in the early 1870s, there were 107 public high schools, but by 1890 that had risen to 278. In addition to my attending a public high school I later became even more involved as I served one term in 1967 as the Kalamazoo School Board President.

At the same time as the growth of public schools in the United States private religious sponsored schools were also opened and families did, and do, pay to attend those schools.

Although public schools are vital, and I have two grand children who are employed at public schools and do great work, I do think private religious schools offer an additional benefit. In those schools children hear from an early age about Christianity. So, if a child's family does not attend a church, they will have an opportunity to hear about it in their school. Although my brother and I did sing for years in the boy's choir at St. Luke's Episcopal Church our family did not attend regular services. Therefore, I did not learn about the word of God, Jesus and the Holy Spirit until much later in life.

In fact, when I was in Europe during WWII, I was frightened but I prayed to no one. And although later I was active at St. Luke's Church with Joyce and our family, I really didn't begin to understand the Christian message until I was in my 80's.

I know now that God protected me in WWII and still does today. I talk to God more than once a day. Thank you, God.

Kalamazoo St. Luke's Church

CHAPTER SIX
Politics in Alpena, Michigan Banking

In 1974, I took a new position at the People's Bank and Trust of Alpena, Michigan with then President George Wilson, and our family moved from Ft. Dodge Iowa to Alpena.

My relationship with George Wilson was always a conflicted one and I often did not agree with his decisions for many reasons. But our stockholders never found fault with how George Wilson ran the bank. Eventually our bank was sold to the National Bank of Detroit as our Holding Company. The new Detroit leaders asked me to try and bring on new Alpena Board members. Traditionally it was George who brought on his friends and associates to the Board of Directors, so this did not sit well with him. We brought on Steve Hier a local dentist and Jim Lafave a very successful pharmacist. In addition, the Detroit bank made some major changes in our lending policies and operating procedures. It was not a happy time at the Bank, but as the real power was in Detroit, they protected me despite a try by George and his alliances on the Board to fire me. After George retired, I then became President of the Bank.

I am grateful to the Detroit Bank for trusting me, and Joyce and I enjoyed 43 wonderful years living in Alpena. And although I had enjoyed the Fort Dodge Iowa bank, the city and people, and our daughter Jan remained in Iowa and found her adult home there, I was glad to be back in Michigan.

CHAPTER SEVEN
Kalamazoo College Music Man

In about 1932, when my brother Bruce was 9 years old and I was 7 our father told us to join the St. Luke's Episcopal Choir, specifically the boys choir. I am writing this when I am 96 years old and over the years I have learned that Dr. Henry Overley, the choir's director was a very talented musician, conductor and teacher, and he was on staff at Kalamazoo College. In reflection we were so fortunate to have had this man as our leader. After his death in 1967, the Kalamazoo College Bulletin issue dated October 1967 wrote:

> *"Dr. Overley joined the college faculty in 1934 and became head of the music department in 1936. He was organist and choirmaster of the St. Luke's Episcopal Church from 1919 to 1944, a director of the Kalamazoo Male Chorus and founder of the Southwest Michigan Chapter of the American Guild of Organists. At least 30 of his chorales have been published. Several of his pupils have had highly successful careers. Upon is death a resolution was passed as a memorial tribute by the Michigan House of Representatives. It read, in part, "As Dr. Overley's personal and professional growth and success developed, he gave rich returns to the people of his community, and of this State. The character, charm and inspiration which he shared*

so generously are his living memorial enshrined with his music in the minds and hearts of all who knew him and among unknown hosts.”

The entire article is available at Kalamazoo College Bulletin (Vol. LXII, October 1967, No. 5) (kzoo.edu)

Our choir emphasized church music, but we also sang classical with our young soprano voices, although I developed my adult voice at about age 13 which meant I could no longer sing with the boys choir.

The boys choir practiced on Tuesdays after school for an hour, and then on Thursday evenings with the men’s and women’s choirs. The boys choir practiced again on Saturday mornings for an hour and then performed during church on Sundays. In addition, the boys choir traveled to Grand Rapids, Michigan and other cities to perform for about an hour with the program including our classical pieces. Our practicing for church garnered us much more.

John Dexter assisted Dr. Overley by playing the piano for the practices. Ironically John was a next- door neighbor of the Richard Petersen family, which included my future wife, Joyce Ann Petersen.

Our boys choir gave an annual concert in the beautiful auditorium at Kalamazoo Central High School, which could hold up to 2,000 audience members with its three floors of seats.

Since its official dedication in 1924, millions of dollars have been spent on the space which resulted in many types of musical groups and individuals wanting to perform on that stage. In addition to the Kalamazoo Symphony orchestra, other traveling orchestras, including from Russia, performed there.

In high school I served as a paid usher and enjoyed seeing dance bands, and individual performers from Broadway musicals and much more. The old school building still stands, although repurposed and renamed the Community Education Center. The auditorium, since renamed the Chenery Auditorium, still hosts local and visiting performers.

Dr. Overley was so talented and knew how to keep young boys under control and interested in the music. The directors who followed Dr. Overley after he retired were also richly talented.

How fortunate was I to have had that experience.

St. Luke's Choir, Kalamazoo, Michigan
John is the blonde, middle front row.

CHAPTER EIGHT
Bosses I Have Known

My uncle Mark Putney, President of the First National Bank and Trust Company of Kalamazoo, Michigan, had a nepotism policy. Therefore, when I was looking into banking positions, he was not able to place me or his son Tim on the bank staff. So, to help me, Mark then contacted Garrett Van Haften, President of American National Bank, his competitor. The Bank Cashier, Abe Deboer, then contacted me and offered me a job, which I accepted. He assigned me to the auditor's office which would allow me to learn operating procedures of the bank.

I was involved in that work for about a year and then moved to a position in lending with Dave Shiner, a University of Michigan graduate and a wonderful person. All of the lending support officers were trained and talented and I enjoyed working with them. I learned a great deal and I also took classes through the USA American Institute of Banking. I was elected President of AIB and was invited to take my first commercial flight to an annual convention in Houston, Texas. That was quite an experience.

Garrett Van Haften was a well-trained, honest banker with decades of experience in Kalamazoo, a strong faith in the Dutch Reformed Church and he took the lead at the bank when it was formed in the 1930s. A few years after I joined American National Mr. Van Haften became very ill and had to retire.

Mr. Cooley and Abe DeBoer were excellent bosses. After

20 years I resigned and was asked by James Duncan, another local banker, to meet with wealthy Kalamazoo businessman Jim Gilmore Jr. to fill the vacancy of Vice President at the Catholic Nazareth College in Kalamazoo.

The President and my direct report was Sister Mary Bader of the Sisters of St. Joseph Catholic Order. She was a wonderful superior and boss. In addition, we brought on another bank officer, Gordon Sleeman who became Business Manager. We both enjoyed working at the College for 3 years. After that time Gordon left for an auditing position in the Carolinas, and I was hired as VP of Commercial lending for the First National Bank and Trust Company of Ft. Dodge, Iowa. What a treat to work for Earl Underbrink and another colleague, Tom Kregel who became a close friend. Both of those men graduated from the University of Iowa.

Two years later I was invited to return to Michigan to be Vice President of the People's Bank and Trust of Alpena with the plan to be named President in 3 years. Although that did happen, the former President, George Wilson, remained as Chair of the Board and kept the CEO role.

As I have mentioned in Chapter 6, that relationship with George Wilson was a challenge, however the ending one was a happy one for me and Joyce.

I now want to highlight the best boss anyone could have. William "Bill" H. Piper, former head of the Flint Bank within the holding Company of the National Bank of Detroit. He was one of my bosses while I was with the NBD in Alpena. He was a fun man to know. He is a humble man and later I found out that he has served as a Trustee for the nationally renowned

Charles Stewart Mott Foundation in Flint Michigan since 1985. He had never told me about that experience. The best part of Bill was he was always concerned about his staff first before thinking about himself. That is why he was one of my best bosses and remains my warm friend.

I had many excellent bosses in my 38 years in banking, three years at a private college and normal army superiors for over 2 years. On reflection in February of 2022, my two favorite bosses were Sister Mary Bader and banker Bill Piper.

I retired in 1990 at 65 years of age.

Bill Piper

"Nazareth College is a Christian community whose members are dedicated to scholarship, free inquiry, open dialogue... who believe in the dignity, intelligence, strength and sensitivity of the human person –male and female– the responsibility of each to develop his qualities to the fullest, not just for self-fulfillment, but for the contributions such development will make to each one's home, community, country and world."

Sister Mary L. Bader, S.S.J.
President Nazareth College
(1962-1974)

CHAPTER NINE
Joy of my life for 67 years, Joyce Ann Petersen Milroy

Here are my thoughts written recently after the passing of Joyce on April 19, 2021.

The summer of 1952, I thought it was about time for this 27-year-old to find a wife. In 1949 I even had to "import" a date from Chicago for my Western Michigan University prom. Her name was Seena and she was lovely and fun. We had met when we were both summer counselors at the House of Three Bears in Green Lake, Wisconsin. But we were just friends.

So, what to do about a wife? I decided to look again at my Kalamazoo Central High School yearbook from my senior year in 1943. Of course, the yearbook included photos of students from the other classes. As I studied the pictures and saw the picture of Joyce, I thought she must have a serious boyfriend by now. I had never dated her during school, or been socially connected in any way, but she sure was beautiful. I called her and Joyce answered the phone. She knew of me, but we really were strangers. I asked her to join Dick Walsh and his date and me to attend the University of Michigan football game in Ann Arbor the following Saturday, followed by dinner. To my delight, she said yes. A few days later she called me to suggest that we go to the movies and get to know each other better before that Saturday game. Which we did. Game day, we were happy to watch Michigan win! We then drove to Marshall, Michigan to visit Schuler's, one of Michigan's best restaurants. The romance began. This was a happy time.

Another time we rode with Mr. and Mrs. Richard Petersen, Joyce's parents, to Ann Arbor to witness her younger brother Jon Petersen perform his required graduation piano recital. The classical performance was excellent. Later though jazz would become the happiest and preferred music for Jon.

Close friends included Lee and Jean Koopsen, who we were with many times. The Koopsens usually liked to take trips to South Haven and Lake Michigan where they later bought an older cottage at the beach with neighbors Dr. Roland Springgate, Bill and Rita Culver and the Hank Barbour's of Allegan. We became friends with all of them. The wives, except Joyce, lived there all summer and the men commuted from work in Kalamazoo and Allegan.

My favorite picture of Joyce in the fall at Prospect St.

Joyce and I attended and enjoyed many activities including community concerts, Kalamazoo Symphony concerts and other local events. We watched the movie Dr. Zhivago in Grand Rapids with Bob and Mary Rizzardi and ate at Schuler's often with them.

After one dinner at Schuler's, I proposed to Joyce. I think it was in March of 1953. I suggested a wedding to be in June 1953. I sure was nervous. Joyce gave no answer, and on the drive back to Kalamazoo she said, "Being married is more than four bare legs and a bedpost." After five days, she finally said yes, but the wedding must be in the Fall, her favorite season, and she set the date for September 12, 1953. After learning her ring size, I bought the two rings with no consultation with her, the custom then. My uncle and aunt, Mark and Marian Putney, recommended Gatlinburg, Tennessee as a wonderful place for our honeymoon. We stayed at the Greystone Hotel and at that time there were few motels, few cars, but plenty of wild black bears in the mountains. We had a great time.

September 12, 1953, St. Luke's Church, Kalamazoo
John and Joyce Milroy Wedding Day

Our first home was an upstairs apartment. The landlords were a Hungarian couple who were fun and taught us practical things. For fun, we named this nice man "Chicky Bones" as he explained that he wasted nothing, using the bones to heat the house. We noticed an odor when bones were burning. We never told the husband and wife any of this.

Our family grew to six. In order by birth first was Jan and soon, Michael John arrived. Timothy James was next and our last was James Robert, on June 21,1960. Joyce had her hands full. She did a beautiful job and raised four nice, caring children whom we are very proud of and love.

Picture of "kids" in 1972

Our children, left to right: James, Mike, Jan and Tim

One of our hobbies was to spend weekends with the Rizzardis in Chicago. This meant fine dining, viewing foreign films, visiting the Art Institute and going to the Tip Top Tap Room at the top floor of the Allerton Hotel where we stayed. Bob and I wanted to visit risqué Silver Frolics where the girls working there usually shed "unneeded" clothing. Joyce and Mary gave permission and joined us!

Baseball and professional football were in Chicago too. Bob did business in Chicago, so he was our leader since he knew the good restaurants and the way around town.

St. Luke's was our church in Kalamazoo, as well as the Rizzardis, and we were very involved. The parish decided to place a mission church near the campus of growing Western Michigan University. We enjoyed helping with that new venture.

Then came 1967 and the Sensitivity Training class in Canada which I was required to attend by my employer American National Bank. That experience resulted in me entering Borgess Hospital in Kalamazoo as a psychiatric patient. I was then moved to the Mercywood Hospital in Ann Arbor for treatment over many weeks. Joyce made many 200-mile round trips to visit me at the Hospital. After leaving the hospital I returned to work at American National but ultimately decided to resign in 1969, as I was invited to a new job at Nazareth College by Catholic Sister Mary Bader and that was very enjoyable and helped me heal. When the College Dean left to be the leader of the Sister Community, I returned to the business world. Joining the First National Bank of Ft. Dodge, Iowa.

As I think about the beautiful, wonderful Joyce on April 24, 2021, I know family was her life. This includes Aunt Grace, Joyce's mother's sister and Grace's husband Ed, and all the relatives in and from South Haven, Michigan. Of course, Joyce wanted to be with her parents, especially her mother, who we later in life called Granny. Next was our family: Jan, Mike, Tim and James. Joyce left childhood past friends replacing them with her new family of six.

One summer, the Rizzardis rented a house at the sandy beach of Palisades Park near South Haven. They invited friends Edith and Bob Crook and their family to join them for a week. Then Bob Rizzardi found a nearby house where our other close friends Dale and Barb Griffith and family and our family could share a house. Now we had a gang of over 20. The four guys departed more than once to enjoy the nearby golf course. The ladies kept things under control. We remained close friends.

My brother Bruce and family moved to Plymouth, Michigan, a bit east of Ann Arbor in the 1950's. We were invited there for a weekend and learned about betting at a racetrack. I picked horse numbers for the daily double. We won, and $2 became over $60. In the third race, the number three horse was Miss Jandon. Our Jan was three years old, so we couldn't possibly lose with the three coincidence and the Jan-Jandon. The horse did not win--it came in third, naturally. Bruce and I arrived home cocky with an extra $50 so out dining we went.

Joyce and I soon went to a Saturday race alone with Joyce studying the newspaper predictions on the first two races. We bet $2 and Joyce had picked the winners and about $60 was in our hands. We then planned a trip to Arlington Racetrack in Chicago. After Friday night fun, Saturday morning she studied the newspapers and again she won the daily double. Then we were not so lucky and lost a few times, but she then picked third place races and won often. Then came another try at Arlington Track, spending Friday night at the Allerton Hotel in Chicago. We headed for the track early, with several sports pages on her lap as I drove. I watched the sky to see the direction planes were headed as my guide, rather than a map. Time passed, and we should be at the track. My watch told me to inquire at the next rest stop. I asked the attendant directions to Arlington Heights, He asked, "Are you going to the track?" I said, "Yes." He said, "How do you expect to pick a horse when you can't even find the track?". We arrived late, couldn't even bet on the daily double and lost our shirt betting on other races, and that was our last visit to a track--no more betting!

Joyce and I drove many long trips in the United States. Joyce passionately studied in advance for our trips. She found several interesting places to visit which I would not have looked for on my own. On a trip to a 94th Division reunion held near Boston, she found numerous stops tied in with the Revolutionary War. Joyce was the educator in our family.

We had one trip to a Rose Bowl game in California which had the University of Michigan as one contestant. We celebrated Christmas in Kalamazoo with extended family and then headed in our car to the Rose Bowl. Winter weather could make things difficult on superhighways with truck traffic in a hurry too, but we made it. Once in our hotel, our paid trip professionals had great seats to watch the parade and made it to the Rose Bowl with time to spare. Joyce also enjoyed the visit to see flowers put on parade floats. The game was won by the University of Washington with a defense that was too much for Michigan. Great Anthony Carter hardly caught a pass, and he scored no touchdowns.

We chose a slow trip home heading south to San Antonio and other interesting southern cities. This trip included New Orleans, which we enjoyed several times, even when the Michigan basketball Fab Five lost in the finals. On Saturday, in the semifinals, Michigan beat favored Kentucky. Joyce really enjoyed that win. And as we walked by the night clubs on Bourbon Street, she felt the Kentucky fans were scoffing at us Michigan fans. Maybe they had downed too many "spirits". She would like to forget the unusual finals, which should have been or could have been, a Michigan victory. A time out was called by an excited player and no time outs were available for Michigan-- penalty so, game over. The culprit took steps prior to the mistake, which the officials should have called, and the game would have been over earlier.

In 1989, we drove from Alpena to Minneapolis to leave our car and take a train to Seattle. Joyce felt a highlight was one of the nights when the train was barely moving in the mountains and actually stopped. Then we watched people carrying skis, leaving the train as others got on board. The next several hours over low, flat land the train travelled very fast, maybe too fast, headed for Seattle. Once there, our rental car was waiting. When the plane arrived with our sons Mike and Tim, they took the driving duties to see the stadium and to meet my sister Nancy, who lived in Olympia, Washington. Nancy drove us to visit in Canada a bit and then her home. To meet ferry boats, she drove with abandon, more daring than I, and I would have been late at the docks. She took us to many very interesting spots.

I entered a contest to win two tickets for the Final Four basketball tournament in New Orleans in 1982. We enjoyed the drive planned by Joyce. She picked the Monteleone Hotel, a beauty, on the south tip of the French Quarter. We didn't know that the North Carolina team, coaches and some team parents would be in our hotel too. What a treat. The elevator near us might hold six. Once in the elevator, star James Worthy was with us, and later Sam Perkins joined us. We spoke and I did not ask for an autograph. Both became stars as professionals. Dukes of Dixieland Band was at the top floor restaurant, so we drank, danced and listened. North Carolina beat Georgetown, coached by John Thompson. A player for UNC, Michael Jordan, a freshman scored 17, and made the final shot for UNC. Our seats were so high our binoculars didn't help--the floor was too far off. Fun anyway.

We won free tickets for the 1983 finals in Albuquerque, NM. This trip would be by train from Kalamazoo to Chicago and then a sleeping car to New Mexico, with Mike and Tim joining us. We did not need binoculars in this small stadium. Our trip included a nice reunion between Joyce and a cousin and her stepdaughter. They taxied us and made us welcome in their city.

We attended quarter finals and many more final fours,

some with son James' alma mater, Michigan State University, the Spartans. Joyce enjoyed all the football and basketball, but how about golf?

My friend Bob Rizzardi called one day to offer his two tickets for a Masters Golf Tournament. He also provided housing for the four or five days of the trip. Fuzzy Zoeller won. The trip from Alpena to Georgia was once again a wonderful trip with Joyce's guidance. Happy time.

She loved the 43 years of home life in Alpena. In her dying days in Saginaw, she said with dementia either, "I want to get out of here" or "I want to go home."

Before we moved to Alpena, both of us had enjoyed Mackinac Island some, but maybe never as a couple. I know the Rizzardis and I were there once. Our family then arrived in Alpena to live in 1974. At that time the bank president annually took the board of directors to a four-day event of the Michigan Bankers Association. 1975 was our first trip and we stayed in the waterfront Dowd House and the owner was the mayor of the Island. That was very nice and at night we heard the clip clop sound of horses, which you could not hear from the Grand Hotel and other places away from the water. We were very happy campers as we had this perk for many years.

After a Grand Hotel dinner, Joyce and I decided to walk the highway on the south side where we could see Mackinaw City. Up ahead as we walked, we saw bright lights and wondered what was happening. We reached a cluster of people and cameras needed to film a scene for a movie. I stood next to a pretty lady sitting on a stool, swatting flies. Out came Christopher Reeve, movie actor who played Superman, and then the woman on the stool got up and the cameras started rolling. The woman was actress Jane Seymour, and the movie was *Somewhere in Time* which has become a cult film.

Many Kalamazoo bankers used the convention to help them achieve leadership roles in our industry. Our president and wife succeeded--he became president of the Michigan Bankers Association. Then we merged with National Bank of Detroit, a great bank. Soon hints were dropped that we should stop going to the conventions. Higher ranking guys in Detroit asked to replace us and so we stopped attending the convention.

We enjoyed about 13 Christmas gatherings in Saugatuck, Michigan at the Mason House, which was a vacation rental. Joyce's brother Bob found this house for us and celebrated with our family. The landlord gave us use of the whole place, including using any food with no stipulation to pay cash for what we used.

Our plan was that since Joyce and I were retired and had time, we would make the longest drives from Alpena which might be in treacherous weather to make it easier on our busy kids to gather for Christmas. Daughter Jan would fly from Iowa to Grand Rapids with a short drive to Saugatuck. Bob Petersen celebrated with us until he passed to heaven. Later the Jon Petersen family joined our holiday fun. One year his mother-in-law was with us.

Many years ago, my brother, Bruce and his wife Judy, celebrated with us. They visited Saugatuck frequently due to the art activities and art school there. Then the landlord for our vacation rental decided to double the rent, so our next stop for three years at Christmas was Marshall, Michigan. There is much history in Marshall. Literature claims this city almost became the Capital City for the state of Michigan.

Next, we celebrated in our living room. Joyce loved Alpena and our big old red barn house. She especially loved sitting on the long front porch during warmer months. But I must confess, I missed being in Saugatuck for Christmas.

Now what did Joyce enjoy about our two trips to Europe? What made it happen was an ad in the paper. Mick Zinsly, the Alpena High School teacher of German, would lead the tour. The two-week trip started in Saginaw, then to Chicago and New York and finally landing in Frankfort, Germany after a six-hour flight. Joyce was nervous about the flight so asked Dr. Bullen to order a relaxing pill so she would not see the ground and ocean below, and it helped. Our trip cost would be under $10,000 in the 1980's. Our leader had taken college classes in Germany, and he was relaxed and had no rigid schedule for this small group and we did not fill the bus in Europe. Our male driver sang while driving the mountains. He was fun!

The first night the hotel was in a tourist town on the Rhine River. The next day we left the group to board a train which took us to famous and ancient Trier, Germany. Then we hired a cab driver to take us for the day to places my 94th Division, L Company of the 376th Regiment fought in WWII in Germany. Afterwards we rejoined our group in a German pub. We headed for the French and Swiss mountains. In southern Germany we visited Munich, Berchtesgaden and the first German concentration camp. Our bus driver negotiated the narrow twisting mountain roads. We enjoyed a musical concert in Austria. Lunch was often prepared by Mr. Zinsly. Our leader had a tour schedule, but he was flexible altering things for weather conditions and other unexpected events. The majestic beauty of these countries was the center of this trip. Joyce had a thrilling time and returned with souvenir dolls and new friends. Years later we took another trip to Europe landing in Paris. Dinner at the Eiffel Tower was fun but neither of us ventured to the top. WWII had nothing to do with this trip. New scenery was the feature.

Joyce was involved in Kalamazoo and Alpena community gatherings. She enjoyed the St. Luke's Church in Kalamazoo and then the Trinity Episcopal Church in Alpena. The Gull Lake Country Club membership while in Kalamazoo was okay, but playing golf held no interest for her.

The first friends Joyce made in Alpena were Betty and John Darnton, followed by Audrey and Elbert Heath. The Heaths originated our "Fryers" Club in Alpena which was an excuse to meet often with these friends and other couples such as Terry and Dotty Carnahan to enjoy restaurants and just have fun! We did numerous trips with the Heaths in the winter to concerts in Cheboygan and summer trips with them to Mackinac Island. Episcopal priest Father Tom Downs in Alpena was a good friend, and he chaired the women's guild that she attended.

No question though, Joyce's life was all about family. Letters of condolence from our grandchildren make it evident.

Over the years when calls came from Mike and Kathy, James and Lori or Tim and Vicki for opportunities to spend time with our grandchildren, she was excited and very happy. Now her vacation had arrived to bring happiness to her young kin. She enjoyed reading to them but her real joy was telling them things from her youth. I was not at her side to hear those stories as she wanted to be the only adult there. When it was time for the children to nap, it was easy for me to see that she had been having fun.

In college, when she told me what had interested her, it was easy to observe that she had spent no time in "home economics" classes, cooking, sewing and whatever. I think she collected recipes from her mother, aunt and maybe neighbor Bertha Dexter. She never made one meal from them that I was aware of, but she enjoyed collecting recipes. We did not starve.

On her own, she was worried about our finances. She was disappointed in what she perceived as my careless attention to these important details. When I resigned from the American National Bank, with a family of 6, a well-used car, some debt, not many investments and no job, she must have lost sleep.

When I decided it was time to marry someone, I gave zero thought to a requirement of a spouse to have quick decision-making skills. She gave me plenty of warning when it took her several days to answer my request for our marriage.

Decisions to improve the appearance of our home on 425 S. Second Ave., Alpena, always seemed a chore. Carpet styles, colors, window treatments and wall colors were all studied with great care and lots of time. I think her decision to have the kids paint whatever they wanted on the front bedroom walls was done without warning. Maybe a grandchild started the whole project and Joyce just decided to let it go. It was fun.

These are just some of my memories of my life with wonderful Joyce who I will see again in Heaven.

Wedding of Ellen Milroy and Jack Frost in Raleigh, NC. December 31, 2016

Joyce in 2018

Made in United States
North Haven, CT
14 August 2022